# YOU'RE A CHRISTIAN NOW WHAT?

## A New Believer's Handbook

*Tracey Mulherin*

**YOU'RE A CHRISTIAN NOW WHAT?**
Copyright © 2018 by Tracey Mulherin

Although every precaution has been taken to verify the accuracy of the information contained herein, the author and publisher assume no responsibility for any errors or omissions. No liability is assumed for damages that may result from the use of information contained within.

| ISBN-13: | Paperback: | 978-1-64398-639-5 |
|---|---|---|
| | PDF: | 978-1-64398-521-3 |
| | ePub: | 978-1-64398-522-0 |
| | Kindle: | 978-1-64398-523-7 |

Printed in the United States of America

LitFire LLC
1-800-511-9787
www.litfirepublishing.com
order@litfirepublishing.com

# CONTENTS

# INTRODUCTION

This book was written with you, the new believer in Christ, in mind. I remember when I got saved there was no information or booklet available to get me started. I floundered and muddled my way through. Even after being saved many years, as people came to the altar to be saved, there was nothing to hand them to help them in their new life. With that purpose in mind, to provide a booklet that would cover the basic principles of being a Christian, I have written this. I thank God that he brought this need to mind and inspired the contents. I hope that it blesses you and is a resource that you can refer to time and time again.

Each chapter has a Bible memory verse in bold text for you to memorize. These will be life-giving scriptures that you can bring to remembrance when you need them. At the end of each chapter, there are thought-provoking questions to take you deeper. I have included insights from my own life throughout. I hope you enjoy this booklet and that it helps you out.

# CHAPTER 1

# AN UNEXPECTED ENCOUNTER

I wasn't expecting this. So, there I was, sitting in the back of the chapel meeting. I was fidgeting and uncomfortable. "Now what do they want?", I asked myself. I gave money in the offering. I attended church regularly. I went to Vacation Bible School. What now? I was kind of angry. Was it never enough? Was there a never-ending list of things I needed to do to please God?

I was at Nyack College in New York, a Christian and Missionary Alliance College. It was summer and they had a week-long orientation on campus for potential students to get a feel for the college. One of the events occurred every morning, we had to attend the chapel service in Christie Hall. On the first day, the preacher was talking about coming forward to the altar and accepting Jesus as your savior. I had grown up in the Lutheran church and this was all new to me. It seemed like just another obligation to perform. I was a good person, or so I thought, so why did I need to do this thing? I brushed off my annoyance and enjoyed the rest of the day.

The next day at Chapel, at the end of the sermon, he talked about coming to the altar again and accepting Jesus as savior. Really?! I thought we went over that yesterday. Brushing it off again, I went about the various activities that were planned for the prospective college students.

The third day it was the same speaker. Somehow, this third day, I started considering what he was talking about. Well, maybe this was not so bad. I could see the reasoning behind this and it started to sound appealing. One of the ladies, on the same floor of the dormitory that I was on, went up to the altar that day. After the meeting, she talked to me. She was glowing and talking about how good she felt. This was quite amazing to me and I was wondering why she was so elated. I was now even more curious than before. I said to myself that if this preacher invited people to come to the altar the next day in chapel I would go up.

Well, thank God that preacher was persistent! Sure enough, at the end of his message, he invited anyone who wanted to accept Jesus as their savior to come up to the altar. So, I got out of my seat at the back of the auditorium and went up to the altar. The preacher led me in what I now know to be the Sinner's Prayer. I was not expecting anything. I thought this would be another obligation fulfilled. Much to my surprise, I felt such a feeling like nothing I had ever felt before! I could only describe it to others as feeling clean inside! It felt so amazing! I wanted to tell everyone what had happened to me! I knew God had come into my heart! I had experienced first-hand what Jesus said in John 3:3," Jesus answered him, "Truly, truly, I say to you, unless one is born again he cannot see the kingdom of God."[1]. Why is being born again an option? How is such a thing available to us? The bottom line is that, *"For God so loved the world, that he gave his only Son, that whosoever believes in him should not perish but have eternal life."*, as it is written in John 3:16 [2].

Have you had an experience like that? I was born again on that day so many years ago. You may be born again too, but your story may be very different. Look at Jesus when he called his disciples. He encountered each of them differently. Simon (Peter) and his brother Andrew were fishermen. They were casting their nets into the sea when Jesus showed up. James and John were mending their nets when Jesus came to them. Matthew was a tax collector. He was sitting in a tax collector's booth when Jesus approached him. Nathaniel was sitting under a fig tree when his brother Phillip told him he had found the Messiah, and to come and see. Jesus comes to us personally, but Jesus said pretty much the same thing to each one, "Come follow me."

Reflections:

1. How did you encounter Jesus?

2. Each of the disciples left their former occupations and families and followed Jesus. When you encountered Jesus did you make any radical life changes?

3. Why is being born again different from being religious?

4. Do you find yourself speaking to others about Jesus? That is known as evangelism. Is that something you have a passion for? What kind of resources might you be willing to invest in, such as Bible Tracts, to assist you in sharing Jesus with others?

5. Spend some time thanking God for your salvation.

# CHAPTER 2

# WHAT IS NEXT?

So now what? Jesus has rocked your world. You want to tell everyone about him. Everything is changing. What you like and what you don't like. What you do and what you don't want to do. Who you spend time with and who you no longer want to spend time with. Is this okay? What in the world is going on and how do you get your bearings?

Let me assure you that this is perfectly normal. Everything has changed, and it is a good change. You have been made new. It says in 2 Corinthians 5:17*," Therefore, if anyone is in Christ, he is a new creation. The old has passed away; behold, the new has come."* [1] An analogy has been used in regards to this new life, that it is like a butterfly. A butterfly goes through four stages of life. Interestingly these can be compared to life as a Christian. The four stages are eggs, larva, pupa, and butterfly [2]. In the first stage, the egg hatches. When you get born again, it is like an egg hatching and all things are new. Next, the larva moves about slowly and eats a lot. After you are born again, you are hungry for the things of God. The pupa is the transformation stage. As a born-again Christian, you are transformed and no longer look or act the way you did before. God is at work in you, changing who you are. In the fourth stage, the butterfly comes forth as a new creature. This is like the new life in Christ where the old has passed away and all things have become new. You're spreading your wings and are flying. In addition, the cycle repeats. That butterfly reproduces and makes more eggs. This reflects that as a born-again believer, you have a desire to tell others so that they too can be born again.

What can you learn from this? Let's take a look at a few of the stages more closely. The larva moves slowly and eats a lot. How do you eat as a Christian? You eat by reading and studying the Word of God. 1 Peter 2:2 shows this analogy between the Word of God and food, "like newborn babies, long for the pure milk of the word, so that by it you may grow in respect to salvation," [3]. We will get into the Word of God more in the next chapter. A pupa stage is a place of transformation. During this stage, the Christian may experience time alone with God. It may involve God pointing out behaviors, thoughts, attitudes, and such, that need to be changed. The butterfly stage is when you fly. Before this stage, the butterfly saw everything from an earth-bound perspective. Now it sees things from above. So too the Christian previously saw things from an earth-bound perspective, but after being transformed sees from God's perspective.

This new life in Christ is very exciting. It can also be challenging. What kinds of tools are available to help you along the way? Let's take a look in the next few chapters.

Reflections:

1. Does the butterfly analogy resonate with you? If so, what stage do you think you are in right now? If the butterfly does not resonate with you, is there another of God's creatures that you can relate to?

2. Think of one thing that has changed in your life the most since becoming a Christian. Compare that to before you got saved. Is it better now?

3. What new desires has God given you?

4. Take some time to journal or write poetry expressing gratitude to God for your new life.

## CHAPTER 3

# YOUR WORD IS A LIGHT TO MY PATH

Picture this. Imagine that you are camping, and it is night time. You need to go to your car to get some blankets. It is pitch black and there are no electric lights. You remember that you have brought your flashlight. With the light from your flashlight, you are able to successfully navigate over tree roots, crevasses in the path, rocks, and other such obstacles on the way to the car. To navigate in your new life in Christ you will need something to help you so you don't fall or get tripped up. Guess what? There is a tool for you. The Bible will be your guide. It is written in Psalm 119:105 ESV, "Your word is a lamp to my feet and a light to my path." [2]

The Bible is composed of 66 books, 39 in the Old Testament and 27 in the New Testament. The Bible is much more than a book. It is God's inspired Word written down by people God had spoken to and through. 2 Timothy 3:16-17 ESVsays,*" All Scripture is breathed out by God and profitable for teaching, for reproof, for correction, and for training in righteousness, that the man of God may be complete, equipped for every good work." [3]*

So, the Bible is God's Word, what do you do with that? I was once taking a class at college that was unique. The text we were using for the class was given to us in the form of printed 8 ½ x 11 paper. The author of the text was the teacher of our class. Her book was not yet published. She made copies of each chapter and brought them in for us. It was truly amazing to have the class taught by the author of the book because she gave added insights into what she had written. Reading the Bible is like that. We know the author, God himself, and he gives us added insight into what he was saying. 2 Corinthians 2:14 ESV says," The natural person does not accept the things of the Spirit of God, for they are folly to him, and he is not able to understand them because they are spiritually discerned."[4] God by his Spirit helps us to understand and give insight into his Word. So not only does God give us his Word, but he helps us understand it.

With 66 books of the Bible, where do you begin? The New Testament is a great place to start. The first four books of the new testament are called the gospels. Gospel, according to Merriam-Webster's 1828 online dictionary is defined as, "GOSPEL, noun [Latin evangelium, a good or joyful message.]". [5] The joyful message is that Jesus came to save us from our sins, to restore us to be children of God. Of the four gospels, which of those is a good place to start? Reading the Book of John, often referred to as the Gospel of John, is highly recommended to read first. John was described as the disciple whom Jesus loved. John was very close to Jesus. He had an intimate relationship with Jesus. Reading John gives you an up close and personal look at Jesus. To compare the four gospels, John's point of view of Jesus was as Mighty God, while Matthew wrote about Jesus as King, Mark wrote about him as Servant, and Luke wrote about him as the perfect man [6]. There are two other books of the Bible that are particularly helpful when you are just getting started. Both of these are in the Old Testament. One of these is the book of Psalms, which are many relatively short songs that are poetic. They really speak to the soul. The other book is the book of Proverbs. This book contains the wise sayings of King Solomon and is very helpful and practical. Wherever in the Bible, you choose to read, I recommend reading daily, and for at least 15 minutes.

Let's look at the gospels a little more. One aspect of the good news is that God himself has written the Bible as an autobiography. The Bible even says in 2 Peter 1: 3," His divine power has granted to us all things that pertain to life and godliness, through the knowledge of him who called us to his own glory and excellence," [7]. How do you get that knowledge of him? You get it through reading the Bible. Do you remember that I mentioned we know the author, so we get to have added insight? Well, we have God himself as the Holy Spirit to give us that added insight. Concerning the Holy Spirit, the Bible says in John 14:26," But the Helper, the Holy Spirit, whom the Father will send in my name, he will teach you all things and bring to your remembrance all that I have said to you." [8]. God also encourages us to ask, as it says in Luke 11:19 where Jesus says," And I tell you, ask, and it will be given to you; seek, and you will find; knock, and it will be opened to you." [9]. So, the Bible is a great indispensable tool. Ask and God will give you insight.

The Bible comes in many forms today. There is the traditional Bible in paper and ink. There is the Bible on audio CD. There is the Bible on DVD, which is great for visual learners. The Bible can be downloaded as an MP3. There is the Bible that you can download on your cell phone. There are Study Bibles, Children's Bibles, Outreach Bibles, Parallel Bibles, Interlinear Bibles, Teen Bibles, Bibles in different languages, and many more. I use many of these formats. What an amazing time we live in that there are such resources available to us. Find one or more that work for you. I encourage you again to read daily. We need our spiritual food just like we need natural food.

Reflections:

1. What is the Bible?

2. Do you have a Bible? What formats would you choose? What free versions could you get?

3. Have you read the Bible before? If not, try starting with the book of John, the book of Psalms, and the book of Proverbs.

4. What about the Bible is most interesting to you? How can you use that to motivate you to read every day?

5. Why is it important to read daily?

# CHAPTER 4

# YOUR PERSONAL GUIDE

Added insights. As I mentioned the Bible is no ordinary book. It is actually alive. How do I know that? Hebrews 4:12 tells us," *For the word of God is living and active, sharper than any two-edged sword, piercing to the division of soul and of spirit, of joints and of marrow, and discerning the thoughts and intentions of the heart."* [1]. One way it comes alive is that the Holy Spirit enlightens us to its meaning. John 16:13 gives us some insight into this when he says," When the Spirit of truth comes, he will guide you into all the truth, for he will not speak on his own authority, but whatever he hears he will speak, and he will declare to you the things that are to come." [2]. What or Who is the Holy Spirit? I grew up in the Lutheran Church and thought the Holy Spirit was a thing. However, the Holy Spirit is the third person of the Trinity. Without getting into a deep philosophical discussion on that topic, God is a triune God composed of the Father, the Son, and the Holy Spirit. I have often heard the following analogy to understand this. An egg is composed of the shell, the egg white, and the yolk. There are three parts, but it is one egg. So, God is three persons, but one God. The Holy Spirit leads us and guides us. As you read the Bible things will seemingly leap off of the page at times. It is very exciting to read the Bible when God himself is bringing things to your attention and is giving insight into what the Bible is saying.

Another tip I can give you is that you can do more than read the Bible, you can study it. I have found the following to be a very helpful method to use. There is a technique called the Inductive Bible Study Method. I discovered this when reading a book by Kay Arthur called "Lord, Teach Me to Study the Bible in 28 Days" [3]. This was an excellent book and made studying the Bible fun. I went through this book with a friend of mine. We learned so much! The basic premise is to ask the questions, who, what, where, why, and how.

I would recommend praying before you read the Bible. Ask God to lead and guide you. James 1:5says,"If any of you lacks wisdom, let him ask God, who gives generously to all without reproach, and it will be given him." [4]. If you are seeking specific answers, you could ask God specifically to give you understanding. Suppose you are struggling with something in particular like anger, for example. You could do a topical study on that word. Most Bibles have a glossary in the back with scriptures that contain certain words, however, this is typically limited. For a different resource, you can use Google [5] to search for the word anger. Another free tool I use a lot is e-Sword [6]. It seemed a bit clunky to me at first, but once I got the hang of it I loved it. I was very impressed with how useful it was. Lastly,

I regularly use www.biblehub.com [7]. I find this to be a very robust site that has a search tool, many different versions of the Bible, the ability to check the verse in the original language, cross-references, commentaries, and more. So, with the Holy Spirit and the Bible, you have a great combination of resources to learn and grow.

Reflections:

1. Have you heard of the Holy Spirit before? If not, you can use the resources mentioned in this chapter to search and learn about the Holy Spirit.

2. What attribute of the Holy Spirit gets you excited? How does this apply to your life?

3. How will the Holy Spirit help you while reading the Bible?

4. Use the questions who, what, where, why, and how to get more out of the Bible.

# CHAPTER 5

# BETTER THAN A CELL PHONE

Communication is very important. We humans communicate such things as needs, wants, desires, likes, and dislikes. Communication can take many forms. We can speak. However, the eyes, hands, and body language also speak volumes. As a new Christian, we can hear from God in more than one way as well. For example, we can read his word, pray, have dreams, and have visions. But what about in the other direction, us speaking to God? How do you do that? Let's compare communication with God to cell phones.

Cell phones are a very popular means of communication these days. Let's take a look at what we can learn from them.

Take a look at a few fun facts in regards to cell phones in general [1].

- Today, nearly two-thirds (64%) of U.S. adults own a smartphone, up from 35% in 2011.

- While texting, talking, emailing and going online dominate, a majority of Americans also use their smartphones for social networking, taking photos or videos, and catching up with the news.

- Smartphones serve as an access point for navigating a wide array of important life events, from health conditions to new jobs.

- Fully 46% of smartphone owners say their smartphone is something "they couldn't live without."

Here is some interesting information on the daily usage of cell phones [2].

- A study recently released by Deloitte found that Americans collectively check their smartphones upwards of 8 billion times per day.

- On average, people in the United States across all age groups check their phones 46 times per day, according to Deloitte.

- Generally, most respondents across all age groups said they look at their phones within five minutes of waking up.

Can you imagine how transforming it would be to check in with God like you check in on your cell phone? Can you imagine checking in with him within 5 minutes of waking up? Can you imagine checking in with him 46 times a day? How do you check in with God? One way is through prayer. What is prayer? A simple definition of prayer is talking with God. It is not only you speaking to God, but God speaking to you. It is a two-way communication. Like the cell phone provides a means for people to talk back and forth, prayer is talking back and forth with God.

The Apostle Paul said in 1 Thessalonians 5:17 to "pray without ceasing," [3]. How in the world do you do that? Does God expect us to join a monastery and devote our lives to prayer? Some people may be called to that, but it is certainly not the majority of Christians. The Apostle Paul wrote a lot of the New Testament and talked to God a lot. He was not just sitting in some solitary place. He got around quite a bit. He went on three missionary journeys [5]. Let's look into this some more.

There are many different types of prayer. Here in Paul's letter to the Philippians, we can see three types of prayer that Paul mentions*," do not be anxious about anything, but in everything by prayer and supplication with thanksgiving let your requests be made known to God."*, Philippians 4:6 [4]. Merriam-Webster 1812 online dictionary defines these three as follows:

- "PRAYER, noun. In a general sense, the act of asking for a favor, and particularly with earnestness." [6]

- "SUPPLICATION, noun [Latin supplicatio.] Petition; earnest request." [7]

- "THANKSGIVING, noun. The act of rendering thanks or expressing gratitude for favors or mercies." [8]

These examples remind me of the traditional type of prayer where you stop what you are doing, get down on your knees, and pray. However, you can pray/talk to God anytime you want. I talk to God while driving, when doing the dishes, or when going for a walk. I have even talked to him while having discussions with bosses, and other random conversations, when I needed his wisdom on what to say.

There is another type of prayer. This type of prayer is called praying in the Spirit. Ephesians 6:18 says," praying at all times in the Spirit, with all prayer and supplication. To that end, keep alert with all perseverance, making supplication for all the saints," [9]. I will get deeper into praying in the Holy Spirit, with more detail in a subsequent book. For now, the short answer is that praying in the Spirit is also referred to as praying in tongues.

The Apostle Paul gives us some insight here in 1 Corinthians 14:14," For if I pray in a tongue, my spirit prays but my mind is unfruitful." [10]. Praying in the Spirit is the Holy Spirit of God praying through you, and it is not a prayer that originates in your own mind.

To look at it another way, we can look at the day of Pentecost when the Holy Spirit came upon the disciples in the upper room. The account of this is recorded in Acts 2:1-4, "When the day of Pentecost arrived, they were all together in one place. And suddenly there came from heaven a sound like a mighty rushing wind, and it filled the entire house where they were sitting. And divided tongues as of fire appeared to them and rested on each one of them. And they were all filled with the Holy Spirit and began to speak in other tongues as the Spirit gave them utterance. "[11]. The Spirit appeared as tongues of fire. This is referred to as the Baptism in the Holy Spirit. This is not heresy. There is mention of this 69 times in the Bible. How do I know that? I just did a search with Google and found this fantastic website, https://bible.knowing-jesus.com/topics/Baptism-Of-The-Holy-Spirit.[12] So back to Pentecost, the disciples were speaking in other languages and those gathered in Jerusalem each heard them speaking in their own tongue as the Spirit gave utterance. Therefore, when someone receives the Baptism of the Holy Spirit there is evidence of them speaking in tongues. They then can pray in the prayer language of an unknown tongue. You can pray in the Spirit any time. I can recall a time when I was working in the IT department of a public school system. I was walking up the stairs and suddenly realized that I was praying in tongues under my breath. It had kind of bubbled up while I was walking up the stairs. Praying in the Spirit kind of wells up inside of you. Holy Spirit must have been prompting me to pray something important, as it was in the middle of my work day!

I cannot emphasize enough how important it is to read the Bible and pray. These are your lifelines. Like an athlete that has to eat a good diet, we eat a good spiritual diet when we read the Bible. Like an athlete and coach relationship where communication is important, praying to God gives that guidance, correction, encouragement, insight, and training like an athlete gets.

I also would be remiss by not emphasizing the importance of being baptized in the Holy Spirit. It gives you power, revelation, and as in the day of Pentecost, when it is spoken, can bring people to salvation. How do you get this gift? Most often it is obtained by the laying on of hands. We see this demonstrated in Acts 8:17," Then they laid their hands on them and they received the Holy Spirit." Then they laid their hands on them and they received the Holy Spirit." [13]. God has it all covered, he truly does supply all of our needs according to his riches in glory.

Reflections:

1. Ponder the analogy of a cell phone and prayer. What one way can you bring communication with God into your everyday life?

2. Define prayer in your own words.

3. Have you heard of the baptism of the Holy Spirit? I challenge you to do a search on the internet to dig deeper.

4. Why is it important to have the baptism of the Holy Spirit?

5. What is the most common way to receive the Holy Spirit?

# CHAPTER 6

# YOU'RE HANGING OUT WITH WHO?

C hoose your friends wisely. This is the last principle we will be covering in this booklet. This has to do with relationships. Some of the people you used to hang out with before you got saved, may not be too enthused to hang out with you anymore. You have changed. You are a new creation in Christ. On the other hand, there may be some people you are not too enthused to hang out with either. Maybe their jokes are not as funny as they used to be. The Holy Spirit inside of you may cringe when they use certain language. You may not like the way they treat people or the tone of voice they use when speaking to them. You may have shared with them about your encounter with Jesus and they may have mocked you. It may be time to separate from some of them. So now what? The good news is that many churches have new believer classes where you can make new friends. If your church does not have a new believer's class, there may be some other churches nearby that do. There is always social media as a method to meet up with new Christians too. However you connect, it is a very important part of your new life in Christ to spend time with other Christians. Hebrews 10:25 admonishes us," not neglecting to meet together, as is the habit of some, but encouraging one another, and all the more as you see the day drawing near." [1]. The day drawing near, is the second coming of Christ. Jesus came to the earth as the God-man, Christ Jesus. He had a public ministry of about three years and then died on the cross for us. He rose again from the dead. However, he will come back a second time in the clouds, in glory. Revelation 1:7 gives a picture of that as it says," Behold, he is coming with the clouds, and every eye will see him, even those who pierced him, and all tribes of the earth will wail on account of him. Even so. Amen." [2].There are many verses in the Bible that talk about the world before Jesus returns and there will be great tribulation. It will be challenging. With all the evil currently occurring in the world, His return is closer than ever. Let's look at a few descriptions of the days preceding Christ's return. Matthew 24:6-8 says," And you will hear of wars and rumors of wars. See that you are not alarmed, for this must take place, but the end is not yet. For nation will rise against nation, and kingdom against kingdom, and there will be famines and earthquakes in various places. All these are but the beginning of the birth pains." [3]. Chapter 24 of Matthew gives a comprehensive view of what it will be like when he returns. Read the whole chapter if you would like to. Times will be tough. You may have a lot going for you in the natural, but we will need all of the help we can get to stay the course, not waver, and not deny Christ. As I have mentioned, reading the Bible and prayer are paramount. The added strength of being connected with other Christians will be an extra help. The Bible talks about strengthening one another in Proverbs 27:17, *"iron sharpens iron, and one man sharpens another."* [4]. Further Ecclesiastes 4:9-10says," Two are better than one, because they have a good reward for their toil. For if they fall, one will lift up his fellow. But woe to him who is alone when he falls and has not another to lift him up!" [5]. We need one another and even more so as the days grow evil. Be encouraged though because Romans 5:20 says," Now the law came in to increase the trespass, but where sin increased, grace abounded all the more," [6]. There will be darkness and sin running rampant in the end times, but grace will abound!

To take it further, mentoring and coaching are very popular. Have you ever considered seeking out one or both of these? People who have a lot of wisdom and experience are out there, who wish to share it with you. This is priceless. People in the business world realize the importance of such people who invariably enhance and accelerate peoples career paths. How much more can God connect you with Christian mentors and coaches who can assist you? You will advance in wisdom, understanding, and skill at an accelerated pace. I am confident that you will be very satisfied with the results!

Reflections:

1. What changes in relationships are you having as a new Christian?

2. How has God made a way to be connected with other believers?

3. What tools resonate with you that you would use to meet other new believers?

4. In the current times we live in, why is it more important than ever to stay connected?

5. Have you considered coaching or mentoring? If so, when could you start? If there are obstacles to participating in a coaching or mentoring relationship, how could you overcome those?

# CHAPTER 7

# WRAPPING IT UP

This is how we do it. So, you had an encounter with Jesus and your life will never be the same. There are things that you can do to grow and mature. The first thing to do is to read the Word of God, the Bible, regularly. Starting with the Gospel of John, the fourth book of the New Testament is a great place to begin. The Bible is no ordinary book. You have the Holy Spirit, the third person on the Trinity, to lead you into truth. This is shown in John 16:13 which says, "When the Spirit of truth comes, he will guide you into all the truth, for he will not speak on his own authority, but whatever he hears he will speak, and he will declare to you the things that are to come." [1]. The second thing available to you for growth is prayer. Prayer, in its simplest form, is talking to God, having a two-way conversation with him. You can talk to him about anything, ask him for what you need, and most definitely ask him to reveal things to you in his Word. God wants us to ask and is more than willing to answer. James 1:5 shows this clearly as it says, **"If any of you lacks wisdom, let him ask God, who gives generously**

**to all without reproach, and it will be given him."**[2]. God wants to talk to you on a regular basis. Adam and Eve used to talk to God every day in the garden before they sinned. What a beautiful relationship they had until sin entered in. You are restored to a relationship with God through the work of the cross by Christ Jesus. You can not only talk to him every day, but he literally lives inside of you. You can talk to him all of the time. The third avenue for growth is connecting with other believers. As you are a new creation in Christ Jesus, there may be people who no longer want to hang out with you. You may not be too comfortable hanging out with some people as well. This is normal and God will bring new people into your life who are on the same journey with you. This wonderful promise is great to hold on to in Philippians 4:19, "And my God will supply every need of yours according to his riches in glory in Christ Jesus." [3]. I encourage you to seek out new believer's groups. I also encourage you to hang out with others who have been Christians longer than you who can share their wisdom and insight with you.

What a wonderful God we have, that has saved us from our sins and has adopted us as his own children. We are no longer separated from him, but God the Father sent Jesus, "to redeem those who were under the law, so that we might receive adoption as sons.", as it says in Galatians 4:5[4]. As you continue in your new life with Christ, using the principles laid out here will help you grow, mature, and have a victorious life! 2 Corinthians 2:14," But thanks be to God, who in Christ always leads us in triumphal procession, and through us spreads the fragrance of the knowledge of him everywhere." [5].

Reflections:

1. What tools most resonated with you? Why?

2. Which tools did you feel resistance to using? Why? Would research into that tool help you understand it better and perhaps see it from another point of view?

3. Out of all of the scriptures, which one really jumped out at you? That may be the first one you want to memorize.

4. Do you think that you could share Jesus with others so that they could receive him too? There are tools called Bible Tracts that you can find online and at Christian bookstores that can be very beneficial when sharing the gospel with others.

5. Do you belong to a local church? If not, I encourage you to pray and ask God to show you which one you should attend. When I was looking for a church, I made it an adventure and asked God which church to go to each week until I found the one I knew was the right one for me.

# CHAPTER 8

# FLY BE FREE

Are you ready to spread your wings? You have just embarked on the most amazing journey. You have accepted Jesus as your savior and your life will never be the same. In this book, I have provided you with the basic principles that you will need to thrive as a Christian. The building blocks of reading the word of God, praying, and fellowshipping with other Christians, will serve you well. On these foundations, others will build. You will have friends and pastors, possibly mentors and coaches, and many others pouring into you. Be wise as you build on your foundation. We are instructed in the word of God to test the spirits. Be like the Berean's and take what you hear and learn, and compare it to the word of God, which is the truth. So now, be like that butterfly and spread your wings. Catch the wind currents of the Spirit of God. Let God lead and guide you where you are to go. He has a good plan for your life. Fly, be free!

# FOOTNOTES

CHAPTER 1
[1] John 3:3 English Standard Version, Bible Hub
[2] 2 John 3:16 English Standard Version, Bible Hub

CHAPTER 2
[1] 2 Corinthians 5:17; English Standard
Version, Bible Hub
[2] Butterfly Life Cycle / Butterfly Metamorphosis;
The Butterfly Site
[3] 2 Peter 2:2 Bible Knowing https://bible.knowing-
jesus.com/topics/Spiritual-Food

CHAPTER 3
[1] 2 Timothy 3:16-17 English Standard
Version, Bible Hub
[2] Psalm 119:105 English Standard Version, Bible Hub
[3] 2 Timothy 3:16-17 English Standard
Version, Bible Hub
[4] 2 Corinthians 2:14 English Standard
Version, Bible Hub
[5] Gospel definition Merriam-Webster 1828

[6] Point of view of Gospel writers, Willmington's Guide to the Bible page 273

[7] 2 Peter 1:3 English Standard Version, Bible Hub

[8] John 14:26 English Standard Version, Bible Hub

[9] Luke 11:19 English Standard Version, Bible Hub


CHAPTER 4

[1] Hebrews 4:12 English Standard Version, Bible Hub

[2] John 16:13 English Standard Version, Bible Hub

[3] Lord, Teach Me To Study the Bible in 28 Days

[4] James 1:5

[5] www.Google.com

[6] e-sword

[7] www.Bible Hub.com


CHAPTER 5

[1] Cell Phone Fun Facts http://www.pewresearch.org/fact-tank/2015/04/01/6-facts-about-americans-and-their-smartphones/

[2] Interesting information http://time.com/4147614/smartphone-usage-us-2015/

[3] 1 Thessalonians 5:17 English Standard Version, Bible Hub

[4] Philippians 4:6 English Standard Version, Bible Hub

[5] Paul's Third Missionary Journey Page 391 Willmington's Guide to the Bible,

[6] Prayer http://webstersdictionary1828.com/Dictionary/prayer

[7] Supplication http://webstersdictionary1828.com/
Dictionary/supplication

[8] Thanksgiving http://webstersdictionary1828.com/
Dictionary/Thanksgiving

[9] Ephesians 6:18 English Standard Version, Bible Hub

[10] 1 Corinthians 14:14 English Standard
Version, Bible Hub

[11] Acts 2:1-4

[12] www.Knowing-Jesus.com

[13] Acts 8:17 English Standard Version, Bible Hub

## CHAPTER 6

[1] Hebrews 10:25 English Standard Version, Bible Hub

[2] Revelation 1:7 English Standard Version, Bible Hub

[3] Matthew 24:6-8 English Standard Version, Bible Hub.

[4] Proverbs 27:17 English Standard Version, Bible Hub

[5] Ecclesiastes 4:9-10 English Standard
Version, Bible Hub

## CHAPTER 7

[1] John 16:13 English Standard Version, Bible Hub

[2] James 1:5 English Standard Version, Bible Hub

[3] Philippians 4:19 English Standard Version, Bible Hub

[4] Galatians 4:5 English Standard Version, Bible Hub

[5] 2 Corinthians 2:14 English Standard
Version, Bible Hub

# BIBLIOGRAPHY

WWW.BibleHub.com © 2004 - 2017 by Bible Hub

https://bible.knowing-jesus.com/topics/Spiritual-Food
Copyright Knowing-Jesus.com - All Rights Reserved

https://www.thebutterflysite.com/life-cycle.shtml © 2017
thebutterflysite.com - All rights reserved.

http://webstersdictionary1828.com/

Willmington's Guide to the Bible, Tyndale House Publishers,
Inc. Carol Stream, Illinois Copyright 1984

Kay Arthur Teach Me to Study the Bible in 28 Days,
copyright 2006/2008, Harvest House Publishers, Eugene,
Oregon 97402

www.google.com

http://www.e-sword.net/ Copyright © 2017 — Rick Meyers.

CPSIA information can be obtained
at www.ICGtesting.com
Printed in the USA
FFHW020923110219
50478110-55718FF

9 781643 986395